Poems of Love and Life for
GEMINI

If you have a home computer with Internet access you may:
- request an item to be placed on hold.
- renew an item that is not overdue or on hold.
- view titles and due dates checked out on your card.
- view and/or pay your outstanding fines online ($1 & over).

To view your patron record from your home computer click on Patchogue-Medford Library's homepage: www.pmlib.org

Poems of Love and Life for
GEMINI
(22 MAY to 21 JUNE)

JULIA & DEREK PARKER

EBURY PRESS

Every effort has been made to acknowledge and contact the copyright holders for permission to reproduce material contained in this book. Any copyright holders who have been inadvertently omitted from acknowledgements and credits should contact the publisher and omissions will be rectified in subsequent editions.

An Ebury Press book
Published by Random House Australia Pty Ltd
Level 3, 100 Pacific Highway, North Sydney NSW 2060
www.randomhouse.com.au

First published by Ebury Press in 2013

Copyright © Julia & Derek Parker 2013

The moral right of the authors has been asserted.

All rights reserved. No part of this book may be reproduced or transmitted by any person or entity, including internet search engines or retailers, in any form or by any means, electronic or mechanical, including photocopying (except under the statutory exceptions provisions of the Australian *Copyright Act 1968*), recording, scanning or by any information storage and retrieval system without the prior written permission of Random House Australia.

Addresses for companies within the Random House Group can be found at
www.randomhouse.com.au/offices

National Library of Australia
Cataloguing-in-Publication entry

Parker, Julia, 1932–
Poems of love and life for Gemini/Julia and Derek Parker.

ISBN 978 1 74275 779 7 (pbk.)

Gemini (Astrology) – Poetry.
Love poetry.

Other Authors/Contributors:
Parker, Derek, 1932–

133.5264

Cover illustration by Rhian Nest James
Cover design by Cathie Glassby
Internal design and typesetting by Midland Typesetters, Australia
Printed in Australia by Griffin Press, an accredited ISO AS/NZS 14001:2004 Environmental Management System printer

Random House Australia uses papers that are natural, renewable and recyclable products and made from wood grown in sustainable forests. The logging and manufacturing processes are expected to conform to the environmental regulations of the country of origin.

TO ALL LOVERS OF POETRY AND ASTROLOGY

Introduction

♊

In this book we have collected together poems which we believe will appeal to readers born between 22 May and 21 June, and therefore think of themselves as 'Gemini' and read the paragraphs printed under *Gemini* in newspaper and magazine astrology columns.

These are based on the idea of 'Sun-sign' or 'Star-sign' astrology – a very recent one, invented in the 1930s by an astrological journalist who wanted to simplify the extremely complex system used by professional astrologers over at least two thousand years of history. But it is all the same perfectly true that you and other people born when the Sun is 'in' Gemini – that is, stands between the Earth and that particular background of sky – do share certain characteristics.

Generally speaking Geminis have the reputation of being the most youthful of Zodiac people, and the theme of young love features strongly here (for instance in Kingsley's *Young And Old* – p.16). Geminians usually delight in doing more than one thing, even having more than one lover, at a time, and may sympathise with John Gay's *How Happy Could I Be With Either* (p.3) and Joyce

Kilmer's tale of *Squire Adam* (p.36). Dryden's 14-year-old Geminian certainly knew what she wanted: 'Take me, take me, *some of you*' (p.11)! Dora Greenwell's *Home* (p.10) illustrates Geminian duality in a different way. Shakespeare's Mercutio, in *Romeo and Juliet* betrays by his name the fact that he is a Gemini (the planet Mercury rules the sign): his *Queen Mab* speech (p.122) shows Gemini at his most talkative! Suckling's *A Pedlar Of Smallwares* (p.107) reminds us that Geminians are great salespeople. And Thomas Moore clearly knew a Gemini when he saw one (*Of All The Men*, on p.106). London is a Gemini city, to which Noel Coward paid a wartime tribute (p.92) and Rhian Nest James's Wales (p.84) is a Gemini country, as is the U.S.A. – celebrated in its best-known anthem (p.118).

These poems are chosen because they reflect your attitude to life, your character and your interests, and also because they are associated with seasons, countries, and towns which are (in astrological terms) 'ruled' by the sign of Gemini. The chances are that you will identify with most of the themes – though some poems we have chosen simply because we believe you will enjoy them, and that they will awaken or re-awaken your love of poetry.

J. P. & D. P.
Sydney, 2012.

To Virgins To Make Much Of Time

♊

Gather ye rosebuds while ye may,
    Old time is still a-flying:
And this same flower that smiles to-day
    To-morrow will be dying.

The glorious lamp of heaven, the sun,
    The higher he's a-getting,
The sooner will his race be run,
    And nearer he's to setting.

That age is best which is the first,
    When youth and blood are warmer;
But being spent, the worse, and worst
    Times still succeed the former.

Then be not coy, but use your time,
    And while ye may go marry:
For having lost but once your prime
    You may for ever tarry.

— *Robert Herrick*

It Was A Lover And His Lass

It was a lover and his lass,
    With a hey, and a ho, and a hey nonino,
That o'er the green cornfield did pass,
    In springtime, the only pretty ring time,
When birds do sing, hey ding a ding, ding;
Sweet lovers love the spring.

Between the acres of the rye,
    With a hey, and a ho, and a hey nonino,
Those pretty country folks would lie.

This carol they began that hour,
    With a hey, and a ho, and a hey nonino,
How that a life was but a flower

And therefore take the present time,
    With a hey, and a ho, and a hey nonino,
For love is crownèd with the prime
    In springtime, the only pretty ring time,
When birds do sing, hey ding a ding, ding;
Sweet lovers love the spring.

– William Shakespeare

How Happy Could I Be With Either

♊

How happy could I be with either,
    Were t'other dear charmer away!
But, while ye thus tease me together,
    To neither a word will I say
        But toll de roll, toll de roll, diddle!

– John Gay

When I Was One-And-Twenty

When I was one-and-twenty
I heard a wise man say,
'Give crowns and pounds and guineas
But not your heart away;

Give pearls away and rubies
But keep your fancy free.'
But I was one-and-twenty,
No use to talk to me.

When I was one-and-twenty
I heard him say again,
'The heart out of the bosom
Was never given in vain;

'Tis paid with sighs a plenty
And sold for endless rue.'
And I am two-and-twenty,
And oh, 'tis true, 'tis true.

– *A. E. Housman*

First Love

I ne'er was struck before that hour
With love so sudden and so sweet,
Her face it bloomed like a sweet flower
And stole my heart away complete.
My face turned pale as deadly pale.
My legs refused to walk away,
And when she looked, what could I ail?[1]
My life and all seemed turned to clay.

And then my blood rushed to my face
And took my eyesight quite away,
The trees and bushes round the place
Seemed midnight at noonday.
I could not see a single thing,
Words from my eyes did start –
They spoke as chords do from the string,
And blood burnt round my heart.

---

1 what could I ail? – what could upset me?

Are flowers the winter's choice?
Is love's bed always snow?
She seemed to hear my silent voice,
Not love's appeals to know.
I never saw so sweet a face
As that I stood before.
My heart has left its dwelling-place
And can return no more.

– *John Clare*

An Old Song Re-Sung

Down by the salley[1] gardens my love and I did meet;
She passed the salley gardens with little snow-white
    feet.
She bid me take life easy, as the leaves grow on the tree;
But I, being young and foolish, with her did not agree.

In a field by the river my love and I did stand,
And on my leaning shoulder she placed her snow-
    white hand.
She bid me take love easy, as the grass grows on the
    weirs;
But I was young and foolish, and now am full of tears.

– W. B. Yeats

---

1 salley – an archaic name for the willow tree

O When I Was In Love With You

♊

Oh, when I was in love with you,
Then I was clean and brave,
And miles around the wonder grew
How well did I behave.

And now the fancy passes by,
And nothing will remain,
And miles around they'll say that I
Am quite myself again.

— A. E. Housman

Girl's Song

♊

I went out alone
To sing a song or two,
My fancy on a man,
And you know who.

Another came in sight
That on a stick relied
To hold himself upright;
I sat and cried.

And that was all my song —
When everything is told,
Saw I an old man young
Or young man old?

– W. B. Yeats

Home

♊

Two birds within one nest;
Two hearts within one breast;
Two spirits in one fair
Firm league of love and prayer,
Together bound for aye, together blest.

An ear that waits to catch
A hand upon the latch;
A step that hastens its sweet rest to win,
A world of care without,
A world of strife shut out,
A world of love shut in.

– *Dora Greenwell*

A Young Girl's Song

Young I am, and yet unskilled
How to make a lover yield:
How to keep, or how to gain,
When to love; and when to feign.

Take me, take me, some of you,
While I yet am young and true;
E're I can my soul disguise;
Heave my breasts, and roll my eyes.

Stay not till I learn the way,
How to lie, and to betray:
He that has me first, is blest,
For I may deceive the rest.

Could I find a blooming youth
Full of love, and full of truth,
Brisk, and of a jaunty mean
I should long to be fifteen.

– *John Dryden*

Carnations

Carnations and my first love! And he was seventeen,
And I was only twelve years – a stately gulf between!
I broke them on the morning the school-dance was
    to be,
To pin among my ribbons in hopes that he might
    see ...
And all the girls stood breathless to watch as he came
    through
With curly crest and grand air that swept the heart
    from you!
And why he paused at my side is more than I can
    know –
Shyest of the small girls who all adored him so –
I said it with my prayer-times: I walked with head held
    high:
'Carnations are your flower!' he said as he strode by.
Carnations and my first love! The years are passed a
    score,
And I recall his first name, and scarce an eyelash
    more ...
And those were all the love-words that either of us said –

Perhaps he may be married – perhaps he may be dead.
And yet … to smell carnations, their spicy, heavy sweet,
Perfuming all some sick-room, or passing on the street,
Then … still the school-lamps flicker, and still the Lancers play,
And still the girls hold breathless to watch him go his way,
And still my child-heart quivers with that first ecstasy –
'Carnations are your flower,' my first love says to me!

– *Margaret Widdermer*

I Know

Oh! I know why the alder trees
  Lean over the reflecting stream;
And I know what the wandering bees
  Heard in the woods of dream.

I know how the uneasy tide
  Answers the signal of the moon,
And why the morning-glories hide
  Their eyes in the forenoon.

And I know all the wild delight
  That quivers in the sea-bird's wings,
For in one little hour last night
  Love told me all these things.

– Elsa Barker

Our Polly Is A Sad Slut

♊

Our Polly is a sad slut! nor heeds what we have taught her.
I wonder any man alive will ever rear a daughter!
For she must have both hoods and gowns, and hoops to swell her pride,
With scarfs and stays, and gloves and lace; and she will have men beside;
And when she's dressed with care and cost, all tempting, fine and gay,
As men should serve a cucumber, she flings herself away.

— John Gay

Young And Old

When all the world is young, lad,
    And all the trees are green;
And every goose a swan, lad,
    And every lass a queen;
Then hey for boot and horse, lad,
    And round the world away;
Young blood must have its course, lad,
    And every dog his day.

When all the world is old, lad,
    And all the trees are brown;
And all the sport is stale, lad,
    And all the wheels run down;
Creep home, and take your place there,
    The spent and maimed among:
God grant you find one face there,
    You loved when all was young.

– Charles Kingsley

O'Grady's Little Girl

Her hair was dark and curly, floatin' to the saddle bow,
Her laugh was frank and girlish, and her voice was
    sweet and low;
When I was one-and-twenty, sure my heart was in a
    whirl,
Ridin' neath the blossomed gum-trees with O'Grady's
    little girl.

And ah! The dear grey eyes of her all truth and purity
What a beacon-light to goodness, such a colleen's eyes
    can be!
They blazed a track to Heaven for me an' it struck me
    like a blow
When O'Grady left the township, just twenty years
    ago.

In those years I've grown and prospered-sure the
    township's half me own –
But my heart's been empty-aching-since she left me all
    alone.

Now we've got a 'Back-to-She-Oak' week, celebratin' royally,
And Nora's coming home again, to join the revelry.

I'll know her by here wild-rose face, her floatin' curling hair,
By the neat black skirt and frilly blouse she always loved to wear,
I've never looked at wimmin since, but at the township ball
I'll tell her all my faithful love-my hopes, and dreams and all.

Oh! the band is playing gaily, but alone I sit apart,
Watching all the merry dancers, with a sore and aching heart;
Gaily old friends greet each other, but my head is in a whirl,
As I watch her twirling past me – Dan O'Grady's little girl.

She's grown stout – she's got a shingle – and her skirt's just on her knee
Sure the girl that I remember's not the girl she used to be,
And the merry lilting music ringing out into the night,
Seems to mock my dying fancies and my dream of lost delight.

Now the band is playing softly – 'tis the waltz we used to know,
And I'll have to ask her for it, for the sake of long ago,
But ah! The dear grey eyes of her, uplifted now to me,
And the unchanged heart beneath them, full of truth and purity.

'Tis a woman's heart that matters, fashions come and fashions go,
And what signifies a shingle, for a shingle sure can grow,
All my lonely years are over, I'm as happy as an earl,
Looking forward to the future with O'Grady's little girl.

– Alice Guerin Crist

His Supposed Mistress

If I freely can discover
What would please me in my lover,
I would have her fair and witty,
Savouring more of court than city;
A little proud, but full of pity;
Light and humorous in her toying;
Oft building hopes, and soon destroying;
Long, but sweet in the enjoying,
Neither too easy, nor too hard:
All extremes I would have barred.

She should be allowed her passions,
So they were but used as fashions;
Sometimes forward, and then frowning,
Sometimes sickish, and then swooning,
Every fit with change still crowning.
Purely jealous I would have her;
Then only constant when I crave her,
'Tis a virtue should not save her.
Thus, nor her delicates would cloy me,
Neither her peevishness annoy me.

— *Ben Jonson*

Go And Catch A Falling Star

Go and catch a falling star,
Get with child a mandrake root,[1]
Tell me where all past years are,
Or who cleft the devil's foot,
Teach me to hear mermaids singing,
Or to keep off envy's stinging,
And find
What wind
Serves to advance an honest mind.

If thou be'st born to strange sights,
Things invisible to see,
Ride ten thousand days and nights,
Till age snow white hairs on thee,
Thou, when thou return'st, wilt tell me,
All strange wonders that befell thee,
And swear,
No where
Lives a woman true, and fair.

---

1 the root of the mandrake, branched, can resemble a human figure

If thou find'st one, let me know,
Such a pilgrimage were sweet;
Yet do not, I would not go,
Though at next door we might meet;
Though she were true, when you met her,
And last, till you write your letter,
Yet she
Will be
False, ere I come, to two, or three.

— *John Donne*

A Renunciation

If women could be fair, and yet not fond,
Or that their love were firm, not fickle still,
I would not marvel that they make men bond
By service long to purchase their good will;
But when I see how frail those creatures are,
I muse that men forget themselves so far.

To mark the choice they make, and how they change,
How oft from Phoebus they do flee to Pan;
Unsettled still, like haggards[1] wild they range,
These gentle birds that fly from man to man;
Who would not scorn and shake them from the fist,
And let them fly, fair fools, which way they list?

---

1 haggard – an untamed hawk

Yet for disport we fawn and flatter both,
To pass the time when nothing else can please,
And train them to our lure with subtle oath,
Till, weary of their wiles, ourselves we ease;
And then we say when we their fancy try,
To play with fools, O what a fool was I!

— Edward de Vere

The End Of The Episode

♊

There is no need to say good-bye,
    And weep;
There is no call on us for tear or sigh.
Men say: *Just as ye sow, so shall ye reap.*
    Is that, think you, a lie?

Now fate points out our different ways,
    And so
We leave the spot where glamour clothed the days –
Leave for those duller worlds that lie below,
    With something like amaze.

No use to curse; whatever crossed
    Our way,
No need for words; when hearts are tempest-tossed –
But those alone may know the cost, who pay,
    And bankrupt, pay the cost.

– *John Phillip Bourke*

She That Denies Me I Would Have

She that denies me, I would have;
Who craves me, I despise:
Venus hath power to rule mine heart,
But not to please mine eyes.
Temptations offered, I still scorn;
Denied, I cling them still.
I'll neither glut mine appetite,
Nor seek to starve my will.

Diana, double clothed, offends;
So Venus, naked quite:
The last begets a surfeit, and
The other no delight.
That crafty girl shall please me best
That no, for yea, can say,
And every wanton willing kiss
Can season with a nay.

– *Thomas Heywood*

The Unfaithful Shepherdess

♊

While that the sun with his beams hot
Scorchèd the fruits in vale and mountain,
Philon the shepherd, late forgot,
Sitting beside a crystal fountain,
    In shadow of a green oak tree
    Upon his pipe this song played he:
'Adieu Love, adieu Love, untrue Love,
Untrue Love, untrue Love, adieu Love;
Your mind is light, soon lost for new love.

'So long as I was in your sight
I was your heart, your soul, and treasure;
And evermore you sobbed and sighed
Burning in flames beyond all measure:
    Three days endured your love to me,
    And it was lost in other three!
Adieu Love, adieu Love, untrue Love,
Untrue Love, untrue Love, adieu Love;
Your mind is light, soon lost for new love.

'Another Shepherd you did see
To whom your heart was soon enchained;
Full soon your love was leapt from me,
Full soon my place he had obtained.
    Soon came a third, your love to win,
    And we were out and he was in.
Adieu Love, adieu Love, untrue Love,
Untrue Love, untrue Love, adieu Love;
Your mind is light, soon lost for new love.

'Sure you have made me passing glad
That you your mind so soon removed,
Before that I the leisure had
To choose you for my best beloved:
    For all your love was past and done
    Two days before it was begun: –
Adieu Love, adieu Love, untrue Love,
Untrue Love, untrue Love, adieu Love;
Your mind is light, soon lost for new love.'

– *Anon*

At Tea

♊

The kettle descants in a cosy drone,
And the young wife looks in her husband's face,
And then at her guest's, and shows in her own
Her sense that she fills an envied place;
And the visiting lady is all abloom,
And says there was never so sweet a room.

And the happy young housewife does not know
That the woman beside her was first his choice,
Till the fates ordained it could not be so ...
Betraying nothing in look or voice
The guest sits smiling and sips her tea,
And he throws her a stray glance yearningly.

– *Thomas Hardy*

Rake's Song

♊

    Who'd waste his sympathy upon
Pale lovers idle wailing,
      When we, for every girl that's gone,
        Find fifty more availing?

    That man's a fool who shows his heart
In public torn and tattered,
      Because she's played a faithless part
        Who never really mattered.

    Anita's flashing eyes were blue,
But Geraldine's are bluer,
      Our early loves were good to woo,
        But present ones are truer.

The fresh and lively all must fade,
      The painted and the sung ones,
      And Time – when *they* are in the shade –
        Consoles us with his *young ones*.

Then, let the girls grow old apace,
    And wander into heaven ...
I'll love a twenty-summer's face
    When I am ninety-seven.

So waste no sympathy upon
    Pale lovers idle wailing ...
For every naughty lass that's gone
    There's fifty more availing.

– Hugh McCrae

Dictum Sapienti[1]

That 'tis well to be off with the old love
    Before one is on with the new
Has somehow passed into a proverb –
    But I never have found it true.

No love can be quite like the old love,
    Whate'er may be said for the new –
And if you dismiss me, my darling,
    You may come to this thinking, too.

Were the proverb not wiser if mended,
    And the fickle and wavering told
To be sure they're on with the new love
    Before they are off with the old?

– *Charles Henry Webb*

---

1 *dictum sapienti* – a wise thought

Jenny Kiss'd Me

Jenny kiss'd me when we met,
    Jumping from the chair she sat in;
Time, you thief! Who loves to get
    Sweets into your list, put that in.
Say I'm weary, say I'm sad;
    Say that health and wealth have miss'd me;
Say I'm growing old, but add –
       Jenny kiss'd me.

– Leigh Hunt

It Never Entered My Mind

I don't care if there's powder on my nose.
I don't care if my hairdo is in place.
I've lost the very meaning of repose.
I never put a mudpack on my face.
Oh, who'd have thought
that I'd walk in a daze, now?
I never go to shows at night,
but just to matinées now.
I see the show
and home I go.

Once I laughed when I heard you saying
that I'd be playing solitaire,
uneasy in my easy chair.
It never entered my mind.
Once you told me I was mistaken –
that I'd awaken with the sun
and order orange juice for one.
It never entered my mind.

You have what I lack, myself,
and now I even have to scratch my back myself.
Once you warned me that if you scorned me
I'd sing the maiden's prayer again,
and wish that you were there again
to get into my hair again.

It never entered my mind.

– *Lorenz Hart*

A White Rose

♊

The red rose whispers of passion,
    And the white rose breathes of love;
O the red rose is a falcon,
    And the white rose is a dove.

But I send you a cream-white rosebud
    With a flush on its petal tips;
For the love that is purest and sweetest
    Has a kiss of desire on the lips.

– John Boyle O'Reilly

Squire Adam

♊

Squire Adam had two wives, they say,
    Two wives had he, for his delight,
He kissed and clypt them all the day
    And clypt and kissed them all the night.
    Now Eve like ocean foam was white
And Lilith roses dipped in wine,
    But though they were a goodly sight
No lady is so fair as mine.

To Venus some folk tribute pay
    And Queen of Beauty she is hight,[1]
And Sainte Marie the world doth sway
    In cerule napery bedight.[2]
    My wonderment these twain invite,
Their comeliness it is divine,
    And yet I say in their despite,
No lady is so fair as mine.

---

1 she is hight – she is called
2 in cerule napery bedight – dressed in blue clothing

Dame Helen caused a grievous fray,
    For love of her brave men did fight,
The eyes of her made sages fey
    And put their hearts in woeful plight.
    To her no rhymes will I indite,[3]
For her no garlands will I twine,
    Though she be made of flowers and light
No lady is so fair as mine.

Prince Eros, Lord of lovely might,
    Who on Olympus dost recline,
Do I not tell the truth aright?
    No lady is so fair as mine.

– Joyce Kilmer

---

[3] indite – write

You Say There Is No Love

You say there is no love, my love,
    Unless it lasts for aye!
Oh, folly, there are interludes
    Better than the play.

You say lest it endure, sweet love,
    It is not love for aye?
Oh, blind! Eternity can be
    All in one little day.

– Grace Fallow Norton

Mock Panegyric On A Young Friend

♊

In measured verse I'll now rehearse
The charms of lovely Anna:
And, first, her mind is unconfined
Like any vast savannah.

Ontario's lake may fitly speak
Her fancy's ample bound:
Its circuit may, on strict survey
Five hundred miles be found.

Her wit descends on foes and friends
Like famed Niagara's fall;
And travellers gaze in wild amaze,
And listen, one and all.

Her judgment sound, thick, black, profound,
Like transatlantic groves,
Dispenses aid, and friendly shade
To all that in it roves.

If thus her mind to be defined
America exhausts,
And all that's grand in that great land
In similes it costs –

Oh how can I her person try
To image and portray?
How paint the face, the form how trace,
In which those virtues lay?

Another world must be unfurled,
Another language known,
Ere tongue or sound can publish round
Her charms of flesh and bone.

– *Jane Austen*

The Name

♊

I've learned to say it carelessly,
    So no one else can see
By any little look or sign
    How dear it is to me.

But, oh, the thrill, as though you kissed
    My tingling finger-tips
Each time the golden syllables
    Fall lightly from my lips!

– *Williamina Parrish*

Kissing

♊

Come hither Womankind and all their worth,
Give me thy kisses as I call them forth.
Give me the billing-kiss, that of the dove,
A kiss of love;
The melting-kiss, a kiss that doth consume
To a perfume;
The extract-kiss, of every sweet a part,
A kiss of art;
The kiss which ever stirs some new delight,
A kiss of might;
The twaching smacking kiss, and when you cease
A kiss of peace;
The music-kiss, crotchet and quaver time,
The kiss of rhyme;
The kiss of eloquence, which doth belong
Unto the tongue;
The kiss of all the sciences in one,
The Kiss alone.
So 'tis enough.

– Lord Herbert of Cherbury

September

♊

You kissed me in June;
 To-day, in September,
There ripples the rune;
 'Remember! Remember!'

We part in September –
 How ripples the rune?
*'Remember! Remember
 You kissed me in June!'*

– Dorothy Frances McCrae

Out Upon It

♊

Out upon it! I have loved
Three whole days together;
And am like to love three more,
If it prove fair weather.

Time shall moult away his wings
Ere he shall discover
In the whole wide world again
Such a constant lover.

But the spite on't is, no praise
Is due at all to me:
Love with me had made no stays
Had it any been but she.

Had it any been but she,
And that very face,
There had been at least ere this
A dozen dozen in her place.

– Sir John Suckling

Ask Me No More

Ask me no more where Jove bestows,
When June is past, the fading rose;
For in your beauty's orient deep
These flowers, as in their causes, sleep.

Ask me no more whither do stray
The golden atoms of the day;
For in pure love heaven did prepare
Those powders to enrich your hair.

Ask me no more whither doth haste
The nightingale when May is past;
For in your sweet dividing throat
She winters and keeps warm her note.

Ask me no more where those stars light
That downwards fall in dead of night;
For in your eyes they sit, and there
Fixed become as in their sphere.

Ask me no more if east or west
The Phoenix builds her spicy nest;
For unto you at last she flies,
And in your fragrant bosom dies.

– *Thomas Carew*

Dollie

♊

She sports a witching gown
With a ruffle up and down,
    On the skirt:
She is gentle, she is shy,
But there's mischief in her eye,
    She's a flirt!

She displays a tiny glove,
And a dainty little love
    Of a shoe;
And she wears her hat a-tilt
Over bangs that never wilt
    In the dew.

'Tis rumoured chocolate creams
Are the fabrics of her dreams –
    But enough!
I know beyond a doubt
That she carries them about
    In her muff.

With her dimples and her curls
She exasperates the girls
      Past belief:
They hint that she's a cat,
And delightful things like that
      In her grief.

It is shocking, I declare,
But what does Dollie care
      When the beaux
Come flocking to her feet
Like the bees around a sweet
      Little rose!

– Samuel Milturn Peek

To Ianthe

♊

You smiled, you spoke, and I believed,
By every word and smile deceived.
Another man would hope no more;
Nor hope I what I hoped before:
But let not this last wish be vain;
Deceive, deceive me once again!

— *Walter Savage Landor*

Love And Youth

♊

Two winged genii in the air
I greeted as they passed me by:
The one a bow and quiver bare,
    The other shouted joyously.
Both I besought to stay their speed,
But never Love nor Youth had heed
    Of my wild cry.

As swift and careless as the wind,
 Youth fled, nor ever once looked back;
A moment Love was left behind,
    But followed soon his fellow's track.
Yet loitering at my heart he bent
 His bow, then smiled with changed intent:
    The string was slack.

– *William James Linton*

The Look

♊

Strephon kissed me in the spring,
Robin in the fall,
But Colin only looked at me
And never kissed at all.

Strephon's kiss was lost in jest,
Robin's lost in play,
But the kiss in Colin's eyes
Haunts me night and day.

– Sarah Teasdale

Poppies

II

Where the poppy-banners flow
    in and out amongst the corn,
    spotless morn
ever saw us come and go

hand in hand, as girl and boy
    warming fast to youth and maid,
    half afraid
at the hint of passionate joy

still in Summer's rose unshown:
    yet we heard nor knew a fear;
    strong and clear
summer's eager clarion blown

from the sunrise to the set:
    now our feet are far away,
    night and day,
do the old-known spots forget?

Sweet, I wonder if those hours
    breathe of us now parted thence,
    if a sense
of our love-birth thrill their flowers.

Poppies flush all tremulous –
    has our love grown into them,
    root and stem;
are the red blooms red with us?

Summer's standards are outrolled,
    other lovers wander slow;
    I would know
if the morn is that of old.

Here our days bloom fuller yet,
    happiness is all our task;
    still I ask –
do the vanish'd days forget?

– *Christopher John Brennan*

Night Thoughts

Stars, you are unfortunate, I pity you,
Beautiful as you are, shining in your glory,
Who guide seafaring men through stress and peril
And have no recompense from gods or mortals,
Love you do not, nor do you know what love is.
Hours that are aeons urgently conducting
Your figures in a dance through the vast heaven,
What journey have you ended in this moment,
Since lingering in the arms of my beloved
I lost all memory of you and midnight.

*— Johann Wolfgang von Goethe,
translator unknown*

The Cynic

♊

I say it to comfort me over and over,
    Having a querulous heart to beguile,
Never had woman a tenderer lover –
    For a little while.

Oh, there never were eyes more eager to read her
    In her saddest mood or her moments gay,
Oh, there never were hands more strong to lead her –
    For a little way.

There never were loftier promises given
    Of love that should guard her the ages through,
As great, enduring and steadfast as Heaven –
    For a week or two.

Well, end as it does, I have had it, known it,
    For this shall I turn me to weep or pray?
Nay, rather I laugh that I thought to own it
    For more than a day.

– Theodosia Garrison

Queen Mab

O, then I see Queen Mab hath been with you.
She is the fairies' midwife, and she comes
In shape no bigger than an agate stone
On the forefinger of an alderman,
Drawn with a team of little atomies
Over men's noses as they lie asleep;
Her wagon spokes made of long spinners' legs,
The cover, of the wings of grasshoppers;
Her traces, of the smallest spider web;
Her collars, of the moonshine's wat'ry beams;
Her whip, of cricket's bone; the lash, of film;
Her wagoner, a small grey-coated gnat,
Not half so big as a round little worm
Pricked from the lazy finger of a maid;
Her chariot is an empty hazelnut,
Made by the joiner squirrel or old grub,
Time out o' mind the fairies' coachmakers.
And in this state she gallops night by night
Through lovers' brains, and then they dream of love;
O'er courtiers' knees, that dream on curtsies straight;
O'er lawyers' fingers, who straight dream on fees;

O'er ladies' lips, who straight on kisses dream,
Which oft the angry Mab with blisters plagues,
Because their breaths with sweetmeats tainted are.
Sometimes she gallops o'er a courtier's nose,
And then dreams he of smelling out a suit;
And sometimes comes she with a tithe-pig's tail
Tickling a parson's nose as 'a lies asleep,
Then dreams he of another benefice.
Sometimes she driveth o'er a soldier's neck,
And then dreams he of cutting foreign throats,
Of breaches, ambuscadoes, Spanish blades,
Of healths five fathom deep; and then anon
Drums in his ear, at which he starts and wakes,
And being thus frighted, swears a prayer or two
And sleeps again. This is that very Mab
That plats the manes of horses in the night
And bakes the elflocks in foul sluttish hairs,
Which once untangled much misfortune bodes.
This is the hag, when maids lie on their backs,
That presses them and learns them first to bear,
Making them women of good carriage.
This is she!

– William Shakespeare

Hermes Puts On His Sandals[1]

♊

Much must he toil who serves the Immortal Gods,
And I, who am their herald, most of all.
No rest have I, nor respite. I no sooner
Unclasp the winged sandals from my feet,
Than I again must clasp them, and depart
Upon some foolish errand. But to-day
The errand is not foolish. Never yet
With greater joy did I obey the summons
That sends me earthward. I will fly so swiftly
That my caduceus[2] in the whistling air
Shall make a sound like the Pandaean pipes,
Cheating the shepherds; for to-day I go,
Commissioned by high-thundering Zeus, to lead
A maiden to Prometheus, in his tower,
And by my cunning arguments persuade him
To marry her. What mischief lies concealed
In this design I know not; but I know
Who thinks of marrying hath already taken

---

1 Hermes, who the Romans called Mercury, was a go-between used by Zeus to arrange his affairs
2 caduceus – staff

One step upon the road to penitence.
Such embassies delight me. Forth I launch
On the sustaining air, nor fear to fall
Like Icarus, nor swerve aside like him
Who drove amiss Hyperion's fiery steeds.
I sink, I fly! The yielding element
Folds itself round about me like an arm,
And holds me as a mother holds her child.

– Henry Wadsworth Longfellow

The Merchant, To Secure His Treasure

The merchant, to secure his treasure,
Conveys it in a borrowed name:
Euphelia serves to grace my measure,
But Cloe is my real flame.

My softest verse, my darling lyre
Upon Euphelia's toilet lay –
When Cloe noted her desire
That I should sing, that I should play.

My lyre I tune, my voice I raise,
But with my numbers mix my sighs;
And whilst I sing Euphelia's praise,
I fix my soul on Cloe's eyes.

Fair Cloe blushed; Euphelia frowned:
I sung, and gazed; I played, and trembled
And Venus to the Loves around
Remarked how ill we all dissembled.

– Matthew Prior

Some Say Thy Fault Is Youth

Some say thy fault is youth, some wantonness;
Some say thy grace is youth and gentle sport;
Both grace and faults are loved of more and less;
Thou makest faults graces that to thee resort.
As on the finger of a throned queen,
So are those errors that in thee are seen
To truths translated and for true things deemed.
How many lambs might the stem wolf betray,
If like a lamb he could his looks translate!
How many gazers mightst thou lead away,
If thou wouldst use the strength of all thy state!
   But do not so; I love thee in such sort
     As, thou being mine, mine is thy good report.

— *William Shakespeare*

From L'Allegro

♊

Haste thee nymph, and bring with thee
Jest and youthful Jollity,
Quips and Cranks, and wanton Wiles,
Nods, and Becks, and Wreathèd Smiles
Such as hang on Hebe's cheek
And love to live in dimple sleek;
Sport that wrinkled care derides,
And Laughter holding both his sides.
Come, and trip it as ye go
On the light fantastic toe,
And in thy right hand lead with thee,
The Mountain Nymph, sweet Liberty;
And if I give thee honour due,
Mirth, admit me of thy crew
To live with her, and live with thee,
In unreprovèd pleasures free;
To hear the lark begin his flight,
And singing startle the dull night,
From his watch-tower in the skies,
Till the dappled dawn doth rise;
Then to come in spite of sorrow,

And at my window bid good morrow,
Through the sweet-briar, or the vine,
Or the twisted eglantine.

– *John Milton*

Miss Melerlee

Sof' brown cheek, an' smilin' face,
An' willowy form chuck full o' grace –
De sweetes' gal Ah evah see,
An' Ah wush dat you would marry me!
Hello, Miss Melerlee!

Hello dar, Miss Melerlee!,
You're de berry gal fo' me!
Pearly teef, an' shinin' hair,
An' silky arm so plump an' bare!
Ah lak yo' walk, Ah lak yo' clothes,
An' de way Ah love you, – goodness knows!
Hello, Miss Melerlee!

Hello dar, Miss Melerlee!
Dat's not yo' name, but it ought to be!
Ah nevah seed yo' face befo'
An' lakly won't again no mo';
But yo' sweet smile will follow me
Cla'r into eternity!
Farewell, Miss Melerlee!

– *John Wesley Hollow*

Yet For One Rounded Moment

♊

Yet for one rounded moment I will be
No more to you than what my lips may give,
And in the circle of your kisses live
As in some island of a storm-blown sea,
Where the cold surges of infinity
Upon the outward reefs unheeded grieve,
And the loud murmur of our blood shall weave
Primeval silences round you and me.

If in that moment we are all we are,
We live enough. Let this for all requite.
Do I not know, some wingèd things from far
Are borne along illimitable night
To dance their lives out in a single flight
Between the moonrise and the setting star?

— *Edith Wharton*

The Vine In Blossom

♊

Along the vines the blossoms thrive,
    To-night just twenty years are mine...
Ah! but it's good to be alive
And feel the veins that seethe and strive
    Like the crushed grape that turns to wine.

My brain's with idle thoughts abrim;
    I wander in a tipsy swoon;
I run and drink the air I skim...
Is it the draught that pricks my whim,
    Or blossom on the vine-festoon?

But ah! what odour freights the air
    From out the clusters of the vine...
Ah! had I but the heart to dare
Clasp something... some one... anywhere...
    Within these wanton arms of mine!

I fleet, as fearful as a fawn,
    Beneath the loaded trellises;
I lay me amid blade and awn,
And on the bramble-shaded lawn
    I taste the wild red raspberries.

And to my lips that pant in drouth[1]
    It seems as though a kiss were blown
On breezes from the tender south;
As though a soft and scented mouth
    Moved down to mingle with my own.

O strange delight, O stranger dearth!
    O! tendrils of the vine about,
O! blossoms trailing in your mirth,
Is Love still roaming on the earth,
    And how may lovers find him out?

– *André Theuriot*

---

1 drouth – drought

When On A Summer's Morn

When on a summer's morn I wake,
And open my two eyes,
Out to the clear, born-singing rills
My bird-like spirit flies.

To hear the blackbird, cuckoo, thrush,
Or any bird in song;
And common leaves that hum all day
Without a throat or tongue.

And when Time strikes the hour for sleep,
Back in my room alone,
My heart has many a sweet bird's song –
And one that's all my own.

– *W. H. Davies*

Summer And Spring

♊

We sat under an old thorn-tree
And talked away the night,
Told all that had been said or done
Since first we saw the light,
And when we talked of growing up
Knew that we'd halved a soul
And fell the one in t'other's arms
That we might make it whole;
Then Peter had a murdering look,
For it seemed that he and she
Had spoken of their childish days
Under that very tree.
O what a bursting out there was,
And what a blossoming,
When we had all the summer-time
And she had all the spring!

– W. B. Yeats

Summer

♊

And sleeps thy heart when flower and tree
Adorn the summer stillness?
And did young Spring pass over thee
In chillness?

Their scent delights and pleases,
On petalled breezes blown,
But in their beauty freezes
Thine own.

The flower awakes, the tree is leafed,
Yet love in thee is dumb, –
Flowers fall, fruits ripen, corn is sheafed,
Ho! Winter's cold will come.

When wakens some November morn
Dew-soft, around thee brightly,
And blossoms on the grey hawthorn
Lie whitely,

Come thou, thy bosom beating,
And learn, through new-found bliss,
No time so joyous, fleeting,
As this.

Come thou, with shadows in thine eyes,
And singing in thy heart,
And learn, 'mid trees, with flowers and skies,
How young and dear thou art.

— *Johannes Carl Anderson*

Words Written In Early Spring

I heard a thousand blended notes,
While in a grove I sat reclined,
In that sweet mood when pleasant thoughts
Bring sad thoughts to the mind.

To her fair works did Nature link
The human soul that through me ran;
And much it grieved my heart to think
What man has made of man.

Through primrose tufts, in that green bower,
The periwinkle trailed its wreaths;
And 'tis my faith that every flower
Enjoys the air it breathes.

The birds around me hopped and played,
Their thoughts I cannot measure: –
But the least motion which they made
It seemed a thrill of pleasure.

The budding twigs spread out their fan,
To catch the breezy air;
And I must think, do all I can,
That there was pleasure there.

If this belief from heaven be sent,
If such be Nature's holy plan,
Have I not reason to lament
What man has made of man?

— *William Wordsworth*

Summer Song

♊

Sing! sing me a song that is fit for to-day,
Sing me a song of the sunshine, a warm sweet lay,
Blue larkspur, and bold white daisies, and odour of hay.

Breathe: breathe into music a summer-day tune,
Learnt of the bloom-heavy breezes and honey of noon,
Full of the scent, and the glow, and the passion of June.

You shall sit in the shadow to learn it, just under the
    trees;
You shall let the wind fan you and kiss you, and hark
    to the bees,
You shall live in the love-laden present, and dream at
    your ease.

And skylarks shall trill all in concert up, up in the blue,
And the bee and the lazy-winged butterfly dance to it too,
While you sing me a song of the summer that's ancient
    and new.

– *Louise S. Guggenberger*

To The Cuckoo

O blithe new-comer! I have heard,
I hear thee and rejoice.
O cuckoo! shall I call thee bird,
Or but a wandering voice?

While I am lying on the grass
Thy twofold shout I hear;
From hill to hill it seems to pass,
At once far off, and near.

Though babbling only to the vale
Of sunshine and of flowers,
Thou bringest unto me a tale
Of visionary hours.

Thrice welcome, darling of the Spring!
Even yet thou art to me
No bird, but an invisible thing,
A voice, a mystery;

The same whom in my school-boy days
I listened to; that cry
Which made me look a thousand ways
In bush, and tree, and sky.

To seek thee did I often rove
Through woods and on the green;
And thou wert still a hope, a love;
Still longed for, never seen.

And I can listen to thee yet;
Can lie upon the plain
And listen, till I do beget
That golden time again.

O blessèd bird! the earth we pace
Again appears to be
An unsubstantial, faery place;
That is fit home for thee!

– *William Wordsworth*

The Horrid Voice Of Science

'There's machinery in the butterfly;
　　There's a mainspring to the bee;
There's hydraulics to a daisy,
　　And contraptions to a tree.

'If we could see the birdie
　　That makes the chirping sound
With x-ray, scientific eyes,
　　We could see the wheels go round.'

　　And I hope all men
　　Who think like this
　　Will soon lie
　　Underground.

– *Vachel Lindsay*

Now Is The Month Of Maying

♊

Now is the month of maying
When merry lads are playing
Each with his bonny lass
Upon the greeny grass.

The spring clad all in gladness
Doth laugh at winter's sadness
And to the bagpipe's sound
The nymphs tread out their ground.

Fie then, why sit we musing
Youth's sweet delight refusing?
Say dainty nymphs and speak,
Shall we play at barley-break?

– Thomas Morley

The Throstle

Summer is coming, summer is coming.
I know it, I know it, I know it.
Light again, leaf again, life again, love again,
Yes my wild little poet.

Sing the new year under the blue.
Last year you sang it as gladly.
New, new, new, new! Is it then so new
That you should carol so madly?

Love again, song again, nest again, young again,
Never a prophet so crazy!
And hardly a daisy as yet, little friend,
See, there is hardly a daisy.

Here again, here, here, here, happy year!
O warble unchidden, unbidden!
Summer is coming, is coming, my dear,
And all the winters are hidden.

– *Alfred Lord Tennyson*

The Poet's Calendar: June

Mine is the month of roses; yes, and mine
The month of marriages! All pleasant sights
And scents, the fragrance of the blossoming vine,
The foliage of the valleys and the heights.
Mine are the longest days, the loveliest nights;
The mower's scythe makes music to my ear;
I am the mother of all dear delights;
I am the fairest daughter of the year.

– *Henry Wadsworth Longfellow*

On Midsummer Eve

I idly cut a parsley stalk,
And blew therein towards the moon;
I had not thought what ghosts would walk
With shivering footsteps to my tune.

I went, and knelt, and scooped my hand
As if to drink, into the brook,
And a faint figure seemed to stand
Above me, with the bygone look.

I lipped rough rhymes of chance, not choice,
I thought not what my words might be;
There came into my ear a voice
That turned a tenderer verse for me.

– *Thomas Hardy*

Song – The Owl

When cats run home and light is come,
And dew is cold upon the ground,
And the far-off stream is dumb,
And the whirring sail goes round,
And the whirring sail goes round;
Alone and warming his five wits,
The white owl in the belfry sits.

When merry milkmaids click the latch,
And rarely smells the new-mown hay,
And the cock hath sung beneath the thatch
Twice or thrice his roundelay,
Twice or thrice his roundelay;
Alone and warming his five wits,
The white owl in the belfry sits.

– *Alfred Lord Tennyson*

At Glan-Y-Wern

II

White-robed against the threefold white
Of shutter, glass and curtains' lace,
She flashed into the evening light
The brilliance of her gipsy face:
I saw the evening in her light.

Clear, from the soft hair to the mouth,
Her ardent face made manifest
The sultry beauty of the South:
Below a red rose, climbing, pressed
Against the roses of her mouth.

So, in the window's threefold white,
O'er-trailed with foliage like a bower,
She seemed, against the evening light,
Amongst the flowers herself a flower,
A tiger-lily sheathed in white.

– *Arthur Symons*

Up The Welsh Hill, And Down

♊

I can still go there.
On a sunny afternoon,
Through the back door.
I'll meet you
Beyond the garden wall.
We'll follow the sheep tracks,
The golden grasses
Tickling our summer legs.
You and I,
Together,
Past ancient enclosures,
And up the breezy heights,
Where we'll sing out
Over the valley,
Then chase the mountain stream
Down,
Cool amongst oaks and mossy stones
Searching for mushrooms and Little Green Men,
And eggs of palest blue.
Lengthening shadows will lead us homeward,
Through ribbons of tidy terraces,

Windows glinting,
Doors thrown open to the evening sun.
My hand in yours,
Not wanting to let go.

– *Rhian Nest James*

Our Little House

Our little house upon the hill
In winter time is strangely still;
The roof tree, bare of leaves, stands high,
A candelabrum for the sky,
And down below the lamplights glow,
And ours makes answer o'er the snow.

Our little house upon the hill
In summer time strange voices fill;
With ceaseless rustle of the leaves,
And birds that twitter in the eaves,
And all the vines entangled so
The village lights no longer show.

Our little house upon the hill
Is just the house of Jack and Jill,
And whether showing or unseen,
Hid behind its leafy screen;
There's a star that points it out
When the lamp lights are in doubt.

— *Thomas Walsh*

Ellis Park

II

Little park that I pass through,
I carry off a piece of you
Every morning hurrying down
To my work-day in the town;
Carry you for country there
To make the city ways more fair.
I take your trees,
And your breeze,
Your greenness,
Your cleanness,
Some of your shade, some of your sky,
Some of your calm as I go by;
Your flowers to trim
The pavements grim;
Your space for room in the jostled street
And grass for carpet to my feet.
Your fountains take and sweet bird calls
To sing me from my office walls.
But you never miss my theft,
So much treasure you have left.
As I find you, fresh at morning,

So I find you, home returning –
Nothing lacking from your grace.
All your riches wait in place
For me to borrow
On the morrow.

Do you hear this praise of you,
Little park that I pass through?

– Helen Hoyt

Behind The House

♊

Behind the house is the millet plot,
And past the millet, the stile;
And then a hill where melilot[1]
Grows with wild camomile.

There was a youth who bade me goodbye
Where the hill rises to meet the sky.
I think my heart broke; but I have forgot
All but the smell of the white melilot.

– Muna Lee

---

1 melilot – Sweet clover

Letty's Globe

When Letty had scarce passed her third glad year,
    And her young artless words began to flow,
One day we gave the child a coloured sphere
    Of the wide earth, that she might mark and know,
By tint and outline, all its sea and land.
    She patted all the world; old empires peeped
Between her baby fingers; her soft hand
    Was welcome at all frontiers. How she leaped,
    And laughed and prattled in her world-wide bliss;
But when we turned her sweet unlearnèd eye
On our own isle, she raised a joyous cry –
'Oh! yes, I see it, Letty's home is there!'
    And while she hid all England with a kiss,
Bright over Europe fell her golden hair.

– *Charles Tennyson Turner*

Upon Westminster Bridge

Earth has not anything to show more fair:
Dull would he be of soul who could pass by
A sight so touching in its majesty:
This city now doth like a garment wear
The beauty of the morning: silent, bare,
Ships, towers, domes, theatres, and temples lie
Open unto the fields, and to the sky,
All bright and glittering in the smokeless air.
Never did sun more beautifully steep
In his first splendour valley, rock, or hill;
Ne'er saw I, never felt, a calm so deep!
The river glideth at his own sweet will:
Dear God! the very houses seem asleep;
And all that mighty heart is lying still!

– *William Wordsworth*

London Pride

London Pride has been handed down to us,
London Pride is a flower that's free.
London Pride means our own dear town to us,
And our pride is forever will be.
Whoa, Liza,
See the coster barrows,
Vegetable marrows
And the fruit piled high,
Oh, Liza,
Little London sparrows,
Covent Garden Market where the costers cry.
Cockney feet
Mark the beat of history.
Every street
Pins a memory down.
Nothing ever can quite replace
The grace of London Town.

There's a little city flower every spring unfailing,
Growing in the crevices, by some London railing.

Though it has a Latin name, in town and countryside,
We in England call it London Pride.

Hey, lady,
When the day is dawning,
See the policeman yawning
On his lonely beat.
Gay lady,
Mayfair in the morning,
Hear your footsteps echo in the empty street.

Early rain,
And the pavement's glistening,
All Park Lane
In a shimmering gown.
Nothing ever could break or harm
The charm of London Town.

In our city, darkened now, street and square and
    crescent,
We can feel our living past in our shadowed present.
Ghosts beside our starlit Thames
Who lived and loved and died
Keep throughout the ages London Pride.

Grey city,
Stubbornly implanted,
Taken so for granted
For a thousand years.

Stay, city,
Smokily enchanted,
Cradle of our memories,
Of our hopes and fears.
Every Blitz,
Your resistance toughening.
From the Ritz
To the Anchor and Crown,
Nothing ever could override
The pride
Of London Town.

– Noel Coward

Impression Du Matin

The Thames nocturne of blue and gold
Changed to a harmony in grey:
A barge with ochre-coloured hay
Dropt from the wharf: and chill and cold

The yellow fog came creeping down
The bridges, till the houses' walls
Seemed changed to shadows and St. Paul's
Loomed like a bubble o'er the town.

Then suddenly arose the clang
Of waking life; the streets were stirred
With country wagons: and a bird
Flew to the glistening roofs and sang.

But one pale woman all alone,
The daylight kissing her wan hair,
Loitered beneath the gas lamps' flare,
With lips of flame and heart of stone.

— *Oscar Wilde*

Neighbours

When you live alone, how you hear each sound!
Should a mouse but scuttle along the ground
And a loose board creak – There! *was* it a mouse?
    Or a ghost's step through the house!

Strange! What fancies come in a crowd,
When your fire burns fast and your clock ticks loud.
Outside, there's a sudden lull in the rain,
    And – who tapped on the window-pane?

Only a wind-blown jasmine spray.
I saw it was loosened yesterday:
But it's odd, it's odd how the fancy lingers;
    It seemed like a dead man's fingers!

Dead; yes, dead. Oh! more than a year.
And what should a dead man do down here,
Tapping like that on my window-pane?
    The freak of a foolish brain!

But the wind, the wind! Like a soul bereft
Of reason, hopelessly lost and left,
It wails and moans. Ah! Years ago
    A voice that I loved moaned so.

Where was that tragic echo caught?
What ails the night? Or am I distraught?
Should I bear the sight, if I saw appear –
    There are steps – hark! – drawing near ...

Steps indeed. Ah! but voices too.
Friends of mine – this is good of you!
Quick! Come in from the wind and the rain:
    Thank God! I'm alive again.

– *Ada Batrick Baker*

In The Train

♊

As we rush, as we rush in the train,
    The trees and the houses go wheeling back,
But the starry heavens above the plain
    Come flying on our track.

All the beautiful stars of the sky,
    The silver doves of the forest of Night,
Over the dull earth swarm and fly,
    Companions of our flight.

We will rush ever on without fear;
    Let the goal be far, the flight be fleet!
For we carry the Heavens with us, dear,
    While the Earth slips from our feet!

– James Thompson

The Merry-Go-Round

♊

The merry-go-round, the merry-go-round, the
   merry-go-round at Fowey!
They whirl around, they gallop around, man, woman,
   and girl, and boy;
They circle on wooden horses, white, black, brown,
   and bay,
To a loud monotonous tune that hath a trumpet bray.
All is dark where the circus stands on the narrow quay,
Save for its own yellow lamps, that illumine it
   brilliantly:
Painted purple and red, it pours a broad strong glow
Over an old-world house, with a pillared place below;
For the floor of the building rests on bandy columns
   small,
And the bulging pile may, tottering, suddenly bury all.
But there upon wooden benches, hunched in the
   summer night,
Sit wrinkled sires of the village a-row, whose hair is
   white;
They sit like the mummies of men, with a glare upon
   them cast

From a rushing flame of the living, like their own mad past;
They are watching the merry-make, and their face is very grave;
Over all are the silent stars! beyond, the cold grey wave.
And while I gaze on the galloping horses circling round,
The men caracoling up and down to a weird, monotonous sound,
I pass into a bewilderment, and marvel why they go;
It seems the earth revolving, with our vain to and fro!
For the young may be glad and eager, but some ride listlessly,
And the old look on with a weary, dull, and lifeless eye;
I know that in an hour the fair will all be gone,
Stars shining over a dreary void, the Deep have sound alone.
I gaze with orb suffused at human things that fly,
And I am lost in the wonder of our dim destiny ...
The merry-go-round, the merry-go-round, the merry-go-round at Fowey!
They whirl around, they gallop around, man, woman, and girl, and boy.

– Roden Berkeley Wriothesley Noel

The Arrow And The Song

♊

I shot an arrow into the air,
It fell to earth, I knew not where;
For, so swiftly it flew, the sight
Could not follow it in its flight.

I breathed a song into the air,
It fell to earth, I knew not where;
For who has sight so keen and strong,
That it can follow the flight of song?

Long, long afterward, in an oak
I found the arrow, still unbroke;
And the song, from beginning to end,
I found again in the heart of a friend.

– *Henry Wadsworth Longfellow*

Tell Me, Where Is Fancy Bred?

Tell me where is fancy bred,
Or in the heart or in the head?
How begot, how nourished?
    Reply, reply.

It is engendered in the eyes,
With gazing fed; and fancy dies
In the cradle, where it lies.
    Let us all ring fancy's knell;
    I'll begin it – Ding, dong, bell.

– *William Shakespeare*

Count The Day Lost

If you sit down at set of sun
And count the acts that you have done,
And, counting, find
One self-denying deed, one word
That eased the heart of him who heard,
One glance most kind
That fell like sunshine where it went –
Then you may count that day well spent.

But if, through all the livelong day,
You've cheered no heart, by yea or nay –
If, through it all
You've nothing done that you can trace
That brought the sunshine to one face –
No act most small
That helped some soul and nothing cost –
Then count that day as worse than lost.

– *George Eliot*

Jabberwocky

'Twas brillig, and the slithy toves
Did gyre and gimble in the wabe;
All mimsy were the borogoves,
And the mome raths outgrabe.

'Beware the Jabberwock, my son!
The jaws that bite, the claws that catch!
Beware the Jubjub bird, and shun
The frumious Bandersnatch!'

He took his vorpal sword in hand:
Long time the manxome foe he sought –
So rested he by the Tumtum tree,
And stood awhile in thought.

And as in uffish thought he stood,
The Jabberwock, with eyes of flame,
Came whiffling through the tulgey wood,
And burbled as it came!

One, two! One, two! and through and through
The vorpal blade went snicker-snack!
He left it dead, and with its head
He went galumphing back.

'And hast thou slain the Jabberwock?
Come to my arms, my beamish boy!
O frabjous day! Callooh! Callay!'
He chortled in his joy.

'Twas brillig, and the slithy toves
Did gyre and gimble in the wabe;
All mimsy were the borogoves,
And the mome raths outgrabe.

– *Lewis Carroll*

Of All The Men

♊

Of all the men one meets about,
There's none like Jack – he's everywhere:
At church – park – auction – dinner – rout –
Go when and where you will, he's there.
Try the West End, he's at your back –
Meets you, like Eurus, in the East –
You're called upon for 'How do, Jack?'
One hundred times a day, at least.
A friend of his one evening said,
As home he took his pensive way,
'Upon my soul, I fear Jack's dead –
I've seen him but three times to-day!'

– *Thomas Moore*

A Pedlar Of Smallwares

♊

A Pedlar I am, that take great care
And mickle pains for to sell smallware[1]:
I had need do so, when women do buy,
That in smallwares trade so unwillingly.

A looking-glass, wilt please you, madam, buy?
A rare one 'tis indeed, for in it I
Can show what all the world besides can't do,
A face like to your own, so fair, so true.

For you a girdle, madam; but I doubt me
Nature hath order'd there's no waist about ye;
Pray, therefore, be but pleased to search my pack,
There's no ware that I have that you shall lack.

You, ladies, want you pins? If that you do,
I have those will enter, and that stiffly too:
It's time you choose, in troth you will bemoan
Too late your tarrying, when my pack's once gone.

---

1 smallware – small, insignificant objects

As for you, ladies, there are those behind
Whose ware perchance may better take your mind:
One cannot please ye all; the pedlar will draw back,
And wish against himself, that you may have the
    knack.

– Sir John Suckling

A Silly Song

♊

'O heart, my heart!' she said, and heard
    His mate the blackbird calling,
While through the sheen of the garden green
    May rain was softly falling, –
    Aye softly, softly falling.

The buttercups across the field
    Made sunshine rifts of splendour:
The round snow-bud of the thorn in the wood
    Peeped through its leafage tender,
    As the rain came softly falling.

'O heart, my heart!' she said and smiled,
    'There's not a tree of the valley,
Or a leaf I wis[1] which the rain's soft kiss
    Freshens in yonder alley,
    Where the drops keep ever falling, –

---

1 wis – suppose, imagine

'There's not a foolish flower i' the grass,
    Or bird through the woodland calling,
So glad again of the coming rain
    As I of these tears now falling, –
    These happy tears down falling.'

– Dinah Maria Craik

The Scholar

♊

Summer delights the scholar
With knowledge and reason.
Who is happy in hedgerow
Or meadow as he is?

Paying no dues to the parish,
He argues in logic
And has no care of cattle
But a satchel and stick.

The showery airs grow softer,
He profits from his ploughland
For the share of the schoolmen
Is a pen in hand.

When mid-day hides the reaping,
He sleeps by a river
Or comes to the stone plain
Where the saints live.

But in winter by the big fires,
The ignorant hear his fiddle,
And he battles on the chessboard,
As the land lords bid him.

– *Austin Clarke*

Vanitas

♊

Laugh now and live! Our blood is young, our hearts
    are high.
Fragrant of life, aflame with roses, all the Spring
Thrills in our windy souls and woos to wayfaring;
And the glad sun goes laughing up the eastern sky.

Laugh now and live! The gods are with us. Death and
    tears
Are dreams we know not. Life, mysterious, divine,
Lifts to our scarlet mouths her young immortal wine,
And wreaths with roses all our passionate laughing
    years.

Only, – remember! The day passeth; not for long
Stays the mad joyance of our golden revelry.
The young eyes darken; the rose petals fade and die;
Sleep ends and crowns our carnival, silence our song.

Too soon the pale hour calls us! Suddenly cold and chill
Dies on our lips and jest, the joy within our heart:
From the loved comrades, the warm feast, we steal apart,
The lonely night before us. Pitifully still

Lie the young limbs, the feet that delicately trod
Life's fluting measures, the red lips that sung, the whole
White beauty of our body: and the startled soul
Flutters and falls before the darkness that is God.

— *Rupert Brooke*

The Scurrilous Scribe

His soul extracted from the public sink,
For discord born he splashed around his ink;
In scandal foremost, as by scandal fed,
He hourly rakes the ashes of the dead.

Secure from him no traveller walks the streets,
His malice sees a foe in all he meets;
With dark design he treads his daily rounds,
Kills where he can, and, where he cannot, wounds.

Nature to him her stings of rancour gave
To shed, unseen, the venom of a knave;
She gave him cunning, every treacherous art,
She gave him all things but an upright heart;

And one thing more – she gave him but the pen,
No power to hurt, not even the brass of men,
Whose breasts though furies with their passions rule
Yet laugh at satire, pointed by a fool.

Was there no world but ours to give you room?
No Patagonia, for your savage home,
No region, where Antarctic oceans roll,
No icy island, neighbouring to the pole?

By dark suspicion led, you aim at all
Who will not to your sceptred idol fall;
To work their ruin, every baseness try,
First envy, next abuse us, then belie.

Such is your stretch! And thus awhile go on –
Your shafts rebound, and yet have injured none.
Hurt whom they will, let who will injured be,
The sons of smut and scandal hurt not me.

– *Philip Freneau*

A Thought Went Up My Mind Today

A thought went up my mind today
That I have had before,
But did not finish, – some way back,
I could not fix the year,

Nor where it went, nor why it came
The second time to me,
Nor definitely what it was,
Have I the art to say.

But somewhere in my soul,
I know I've met the thing before;
It just reminded me – 'twas all –
And came my way no more.

– *Emily Dickinson*

The Star-Spangled Banner

♊

Oh, say, can you see, by the dawn's early light,
What so proudly we hailed at the twilight's last
   gleaming?
Whose broad stripes and bright stars, thru the perilous
   fight,
O'er the ramparts we watched, were so gallantly
   streaming?
And the rockets' red glare, the bombs bursting in air,
Gave proof through the night that our flag was still
   there.
O say, does that star-spangled banner yet wave
O'er the land of the free and the home of the brave?

On the shore dimly seen through the mists of the deep,
Where the foe's haughty host in dread silence reposes,
What is that which the breeze, o'er the towering steep,
As it fitfully blows, half conceals, half discloses?
Now it catches the gleam of the morning's first beam,
In full glory reflected, now shines on the stream:
Tis the star-spangled banner: O, long may it wave
O'er the land of the free and the home of the brave!

And where is that band who so vauntingly swore
That the havoc of war and the battle's confusion
A home and a country should leave us no more?
Their blood has washed out their foul footsteps' pollution.
No refuge could save the hireling and slave
From the terror of flight or the gloom of the grave:
And the star-spangled banner in triumph doth wave
O'er the land of the free and the home of the brave.

O, thus be it ever when freemen shall stand,
Between their loved home and the war's desolation!
Blest with victory and peace, may the heaven-rescued land
Praise the Power that hath made and preserved us a nation!
Then conquer we must, when our cause it is just,
And this be our motto: 'In God is our trust'
And the star-spangled banner in triumph shall wave
O'er the land of the free and the home of the brave!

– Frances Scott Key

An Astrologer's Song

♊

To the Heavens above us
Oh, look and behold
The planets that love us
All harnessed in gold!
What chariots, what horses,
Against us shall bide
While the Stars in their courses
Do fight on our side?

All thought, all desires,
That are under the sun,
Are one with their fires,
As we also are one;
All matter, all spirit,
All fashion, all frame,
Receive and inherit
Their strength from the same.

Earth quakes in her throes
And we wonder for why!
But the blind planet knows
When her ruler is nigh;
And, attuned since Creation,
To perfect accord,
She thrills in her station
And yearns to her Lord.

Then, doubt not, ye fearful –
The Eternal is King –
Up, heart, and be cheerful,
And lustily sing:
What chariots, what horses,
Against us shall bide
While the Stars in their courses
Do fight on our side?

– *Rudyard Kipling*

Not From The Stars ...

Not from the stars do I my judgment pluck;
And yet methinks I have astronomy,
But not to tell of good or evil luck,
Of plagues, of dearths, or seasons' quality;
Nor can I fortune to brief minutes tell,
Pointing to each his thunder, rain and wind,
Or say with princes if it shall go well,
By oft predict that I in heaven find:
But from thine eyes my knowledge I derive,
And, constant stars, in them I read such art
As truth and beauty shall together thrive,
If from thyself to store thou wouldst convert;
Or else of thee this I prognosticate:
Thy end is truth's and beauty's doom and date.

– *William Shakespeare*

Index

Anderson, Johannes Carl	Summer	71
Anon	The Unfaithful Shepherdess	27
Austen, Jane	Mock Panegyric On A Young Friend	40
Baker, Ada Batrick	Neighbours	97
Barker, Ella	I Know	14
Bourke, John Philip	The End Of The Episode	25
Brennan, Christopher John	Poppies	53
Brooke, Rupert	Vanitas	114
Carew, Thomas	Ask Me No More	46
Clare, John	First Love	5
Clarke, Austin	The Scholar	112
Carroll, Lewis	Jabberwocky	105
Coward, Noel	London Pride	93
Craik, Dinah Maria	A Silly Song	110
Crist, Alice Guerin	O'Grady's Little Girl	17
Davies, W. H.	When On A Summer's Morn	69
De Vere, Edward	A Renunciation	23
Dickinson, Emily	A Thought Went Up My Mind Today	118
Donne, John	Go And Catch A Falling Star	21
Dryden, John	A Young Girl's Song	11
Eliot, George	Count The Day Lost	104
Freneau, Philip	The Scurrilous Scribe	116
Garrison, Theodosia	The Cynic	56

Gay, John	How Happy Could I Be With Either	3
	Our Polly Is A Sad Slut	15
Goethe, Johann Wolfgang von	Night Thoughts	55
Greenwell, Dora	Home	10
Guggenberger, Louise S.	Summer Song	75
Hardy, Thomas	At Tea	29
	On Midsummer Eve	82
Hart, Lorenz	It Never Entered My Mind	34
Herbert, Lord	Kissing	43
Herrick, Robert	To Virgins To Make Much Of Time	1
Heywood, Thomas	She That Denies Me I Would Have	26
Hollow, John Wesley	Miss Melerlee	65
Hoyt, Helen	Ellis Park	88
Hunt, Leigh	Jenny Kiss'd Me	33
Houseman, A. E.	When I Was One-And-Twenty	4
	O When I Was In Love With You	8
Jonson, Ben	His Supposed Mistress	20
Key, Frances Scott	The Star-Spangled Banner	119
Kilmer, Joyce	Squire Adam	37
Kingsley, Charles	Young And Old	16
Kipling, Rudyard	An Astrologer's Song	121
Landor, Walter Savage	To Ianthe	50
Lee, Muna	Behind The House	90
Lindsay, Vachel	The Horrid Voice Of Science	78
Linton, William James	Love And Youth	51
Longfellow, Henry Wadsworth	Hermes Puts On His Sandals	59
	The Poet's Calendar: June	81
	The Arrow And The Song	102
McCrae, Dorothy Frances	September	44
McCrae, Hugh	Rake's Song	30

Loved the book?

Join thousands of other readers online at

AUSTRALIAN READERS:

randomhouse.com.au/talk

NEW ZEALAND READERS:

randomhouse.co.nz/talk

Milton, John	From L'allegro	63
Moore, Thomas	Of All The Men	107
Morley, Thomas	Now Is The Month Of Maying	79
Nest James, Rhian	Up The Welsh Hill, And Down	85
Noel, Roden Berkeley Wriothesley	The Merry-Go-Round	100
Norton, Grace Fallow	You Say There Is No Love	39
O'Reilly, John Boyle	A White Rose	36
Parrish, Williamina	The Name	42
Peek, Samuel Milturn	Dollie	48
Prior, Matthew	The Merchant, To Secure His Treasure	61
Shakespeare, William	It Was A Lover And His Lass	2
	Some Say Thy Fault Is Youth	62
	Tell Me, Where Is Fancy Bred?	103
	Queen Mab	57
	Not From The Stars . . .	123
Suckling, Sir John	Out Upon It	45
	A Pedlar Of Smallwares	108
Symons, Arthur	At Glan-Y-Wern	84
Teasdale, Sarah	The Look	52
Lord Tennyson, Alfred	The Throstle	80
	Song – The Owl	83
Theuriot, Andre	The Vine In Blossom	67
Thompson, James	In The Train	99
Turner, Charles Tennyson	Letty's Globe	91
Walsh, Thomas	Our Little House	87
Webb, Charles Henry	*Dictum Sapienti*	32
Wharton, Edith	Yet For One Rounded Moment	66
Widdermer, Margaret	Carnations	12
Wilde, Oscar	*Impression Du Matin*	96

Wordsworth, William	Words Written In Early Spring	73
	To The Cuckoo	76
	Upon Westminster Bridge	92
Yeats, W. B.	An Old Song Re-Sung	7
	Girl's Song	9
	Summer And Spring	70

Derek & Julia Parker

Derek and Julia Parker became internationally famous with the publication of *The Compleat Astrologer* in 1971, the first thorough modern text-book of astrology. A world-wide best-seller, with a new edition released in 1984, it remained in print for twenty years until replaced by *Parkers' Astrology*. Julia Parker remains an active astrologer; Derek (who for five years edited the UK's *Poetry Review*) is also a biographer. They have jointly written books on dream interpretation, popular psychology, travel, the theatre, magic – and love. In 2002, after forty years of working in London, they emigrated to Sydney, where they live with their two wire-haired terriers, Fille and Crim.